AN ALPHABETIC COLLECTION

AN ALPHABETIC COLLECTION OF RIDICULOUS MEDICAL POETRY

AND

A DEVIL'S DICTIONARY OF MEDICAL SPECIALISTS

ABC

Joel Berman

PENNYWYSE PRESS
TUCSON, ARIZONA

Copyright © 2010 by Joel Berman

All rights reserved. No part of this book may be reproduced or transmitted in any form or by any means, electronic or mechanical, including photocopying, recording or by any information storage and retrieval system, without written permission from the author, except for the inclusion of a brief quotation in a review.

Published in the United States of America by:

Pennywyse Press
3710 East Edison Street
Tucson, AZ 85716

Library of Congress Control Number: 2010922829

ISBN 978-1-935437-17-8
ISBN 1-935437-17-8

Book and Cover Design by Leila Joiner
Cover illustration: doctor © caraman

Printed in the United States of America on Acid-Free Paper

The best of all physicians
Is apple pie and cheese

—Eugene Field

The Appendix was made by the Lord, on day eight,
He was tired, and bored, and didn't feel great!
'Twas made to send surgeons' young children to college,
And fill daughters' rooms up with rare Barbie Dollage.

Valentino passed on, when his ruptured one day,
His tomb is still hounded by women, they say.
And history's filled with stories to chide us,
Of many who perished with appendicitis.

So, for centuries, barbers and surgeons alike
Filleted open persons, with a blade or a spike.
And those who survived underneath the sharp knife
Were terribly scarred for the rest of their life.

Now doctors, with x-rays and blood counts, with ease
Can diagnose this, a most common disease.
You needn't succumb to a phlegmonous "appy,"
You just need to make an old surgeon quite happy.

So the next time you feel a great cramp in your belly,
And you're nauseous…vomiting stuff that's quite smelly,
Go to the doctor who handles the knife,
He may just be able to salvage your life.

Abortionist – A person with a solution to overpopulation

Acupuncturist – A physician who is good at starting IV's

Alcoholic – A doctor who has found a place to go when being sued too often

Allergist – A physician who only knows how to use Benedryl and steroids

Alternative Medicine – A specialty that has found a good use for discarded shark cartilage, oil of witch's tooth, and other such nostrums

Alzheimer's Specialist – A doctor who…a doctor who…a doctor…a…

American College (of Surgeons, Internists, Obstetricians, Gynecologists, etc.) – Groups that ennoble themselves with fancy, framed wall documents to enhance physician's offices

Anatomist – Doctor who likes the smell of formaldehyde

Anesthesiologist – A person who is not vilified for passing gas in public

Angiographer – Usually, a cardiologist bored with reading EKG's

Apothecary – A person who is in the drug trade, legal or otherwise

Audiologist – What? WHAT? WHAT?

I think that I shall never see,
A tree as lovely as a Breast,
A Breast that blossoms in its youth
Upon a woman's heaving chest.
To nurture children, to flaunt, to pose,
Like gentle petals of a rose.

Trees are made for wood and paper
At industrialists' behest,
But only God and Plastic Surgeons
Can make a lovely woman's Breast.

Bacteriologist – Opposite of Fronteriologist

Berman, Joel A. – A wannabe writer who was a Theatre Arts and English Major in college and somehow ended up as a surgeon

Biochemist – Man who works with opium poppies

Biologist – One who plays with *biols* (whatever *biols* are)

Brain Surgeon – A doctor whose patients rarely speak to him

Breast Surgeon – A surgeon who doesn't eat the dark meat of a chicken

Why in the world do we each have a colon?
Don't need it for business or dancin' or bowlin'.
They say it absorbs all the water we drink,
But, oh, how the contents just normally stink!

And sometimes it's surgically brought to the skin,
(A circumstance most would not like to be in).
Called a colostomy, it's opening a stoma,
(Not quite the thing for an epic by Homer)!

And when at inopportune times, things get "rollin',"
Then know that you're getting a note from your colon.
And you better take care…and heed my advice,
Or you'll fill your surroundings with stale-smelling "spice."

So watch what you eat, and don't swallow much air,
And get your relief…when others aren't there.
'Cause when those big bells in your stomach start tollin',
You just may not know if you're comin' or colon!

Cancer Specialist – A physician who tries to cure by giving poisons

Cardiologist – A doctor who treats heart disease patients and displays photographs on the wall of his office showing himself running a marathon

Carter, Dr. Samuel of Erie Pennsylvania – Famous discoverer in 1868 of Little Liver Pills, a remedy for feeling "down-and-out, blue, down-in-the-dumps, depressed, worn out, sunk, logy, sluggish, all in, listless, mean, cranky, peevish, low, cross, tired, stuffy, heavy, miserable, run down, gloomy, what's-the-use, sullen, as well as sick, headache, torpid liver, indigestion, constipation or what-ails-you"

Chemist – A specialist who works in Cali, Colombia

Clinicians – Doctors who can actually make a diagnosis without running tests worth $20,000

Complementary Medicine – Telling a suffering person he or she looks good

Cosmetic Surgeon – A physician who wants to make the exorbitant salary of a plastic surgeon by doing highly remunerative procedures like breast implants, but hasn't got the credentials or training and needs some label to put after his name

Criminal – An enterprising doctor who makes a bundle by giving prescriptions for narcotics to anyone who so desires

Cytologist – A doctor who can't stand patients, so ensconces himself at a microscope eight hours a day

Whenever I have Diarrhea,
I think of the horses at Hiarrhea!

Darwinian – A very old physician with a long white beard, who is sometimes depicted as an ape

Dead – An alternative to alive, often shunned by patients

Dentist – A doctor trained to ask questions of patients who can't answer them

Dermatologist – Pimple squeezer with a degree

Diabetologist – A warrior in the struggle against Dunkin Donuts

Diagnostician – A doctor who can diagnose disease using several million dollars worth of tests

Dietitian – A fat person who tells others how to lose weight

Doctor – What every Jewish mother wants for her daughter

Druggist – See chemist

Think about Eyes, most people have two,
Some are crossed, some bloodshot, some brown, and some blue.
The farsighted ones can see miles at a glance,
The nearsighted myopes can look down their pants.

When you can't see your toilet and pee on the floor,
It's time to go visit the "eye-doc" next door.
He'll treat you with lasers and bring back your vision,
Once you have made that expensive decision.

But remember the old days, when out of his pocket,
A salesman would pull a fake eye for your socket.
Instead of just contacts to change your eye color,
You could change the whole eye for less than a dollar!

As the times have rolled by, the eye-docs have rolled too,
They are advertised much like an ophthalmic zoo.
And beware of the eye-doc who sends, postage due,
A card that says, "I'll keep an eye out for you!"

Eccentric – A medical specialist

Egotist – Same as Eccentric

Electron Microscopist – A physician who pretends he sees something

Embryologist – One specializing in an extreme form of medicine, where smaller is better

Emergency Medicine Physician – A doctor trained in making patients wait long hours to be seen for unnecessary ailments

Endocrinologist – A doctor who supplies special medications to baseball and football players to enhance their performance

Epidemiologist – A physician who catches sexual predators

Experimentalists – Most physicians who deal with difficult diseases

Eye Doctor – A doctor with a very limited/localized knowledge of anatomy, with an office replete with huge machines for reading letters on a chart

As we take on years, we get older and bolder.
Our urges get warmer…control gets much colder!
We no longer hear the sweet music *delectum,*
The symphonic discharge that sings from our rectum.

We know what's occurring and think we are sneaking,
But others around us know well that we're leaking!
When, as guests, we are rising and slowly departing,
The host turns his nose, as we start in to Farting.

I think we should change all the rules of decorum,
By assembling a National Flatulence Forum.
To redefine etiquette, in the manner of Sartre,
And soon we will all be admiring the Fartre.

Family Doctor – A person to see for sleeping pills and Viagra

Fake – See Quack

Female Doctor – A physician who signs her name with two X's

Fetal Medicine – See veterinary medicine

Foot Doctor – An inch doctor who has done twelve procedures

Freudian – A specialist with a vocabulary limited to *I see* and *hmm*

We've all heard of diamonds and rubies and pearls,
The glistening jewels of women and girls.
But there's one kind of stone that the surgeons collect,
That gemologists may have, but never inspect.

These stones may be yellow, or green, or with facets,
But the owner does not ever increase her assets.
For having them only gives suffering and pain,
Like the curse of a diamond from a statue in Spain!

We can often accuse our ancestors for genes
That gave us these awful pain-making machines.
And you never will find this Gallstone epiphany
In any display case or window at Tiffany!

So let us pay homage to this jewel with such vices,
That gives owners pain when they eat fat and spices.
And praise to the surgeon (I hope you'll respect me)
When I say that you need…a cholecystectomy.

Gastroenterologist – A doctor who revels in sticking tubes in private places

General Surgeon – another term for the Almighty, a legend in his own mind

Geneticist – A wise man who can tell the difference between men and women

Grandfather Clause doctors – Unqualified physicians practicing because they knew Noah

Group Medicine Physicians – Physicians who tried unsuccessfully to practice as private practitioners

Hemorrhoids are a pain in the ---,
To scratch them in public demonstrates no class.
Showing them to doctors is very embarrassing.
I'd rather treat them with Plaster of Paris-ing

And nothing, I find, in public offends
As seeing a panty bulge – *Depends*.
Hemorrhoids (I believe, to be on the level)
Weren't made by God, but by the Devil.

Heart Doctor – See cardiologist

Hematologist – Cohort of She-matologist

Herpetologist – Similar to above, female possessive

Hepatologist – A physician who never eats liver and onions

Histologist – See herpetologist, similar but different sex

Holistic – Found in a hole

Hospitalist – A doctor who can't afford his own office

House staff – Young doctors-in-training who practice medicine in the truest meaning of the word *practice*, on indigent patients unable to pay for real, well-trained doctors

It takes a well-planned, bold decision
To make a surgical Incision.
The sword is mightier than the pen
To get inside the skin…and then,
It also takes more than a pen
To close the damn thing up again!

Internist – One who stands in line for his patients

Incompetent Doctors – Physicians who specialize in procedures they enjoy, but in which they have no formal training (see Quack)

Infectious Disease Doctors – Physicians who love purulence

Elbow, knee, shoulder, and talo-navicular,
Along with the wrist, all have one thing particular.
They all are the foci at some times and points
Of being what we call...disreputable Joints!

You can splint 'em and cast 'em, inject 'em with steroids,
And worry so much that you'll soon have large hemorrhoids!
Then you will be x-rayed from guzzle to zatch,
And even some places you can't even scratch!

And when all the tests have been ordered and done,
You'll be ready to comply like a young novice nun.
They'll scope you and poke you and start with orthotics,
And send you to therapists treating neurotics!

And just when you think that you've gone through the worst,
The *fun* part will end, and your bubble will burst.
And the next step, they'll claim, without malice or perjury,
"I'm afraid, dear patient, you will need major surgery!"

So you get six opinions, different and various,
Proposing procedures that sound quite nefarious.
And finally resistance wears out, and you're able
To consent to lie down on a surgical table!

And when all the surgery's done, and time passes,
With pain medication and exercise classes,

You're no better off than the first day you started,
And glad that the damn old M.D. has departed.

You sit in a corner…you think and you ponder.
Maybe the pain's not so bad, and you wonder,
*I should have just left the damn joint ill at ease,
'Cause the cure's been much worse than the friggin' disease!*

Juvenile Doctors – M.D.'s who have not yet gone through puberty

Jungian Psychiatrist – Nobody knows what this doctor does…in fact, he does not know what he does

K I'd much rather fall and break some bones,
Than live my life with Kidney stones.
For if you have patience, the fractures will heal,
And soon you'll proclaim, *it's not such a big deal!*

But the Kidney stones seem to come back, file and rank,
And you just can't be sure that that pain in your flank
Won't come back soon, tomorrow, next week, or next year,
And you'll live all your life in frank horror and fear.

But I have the answer for those with compliance,
By acting according to cold, rigid science.
Stop being a whiner, and crier, and moaner,
By quickly becoming a two-kidney donor!

Krock – See Quack

Kinsey – Dr. who brought sex to America

Kildare – Eminent television brain surgeon without an M.D. degree and no bedside manner

If you've been smoking cigarettes,
I'm ready to accept all bets,
'Cause odds are high you'll soon contract
Some bad disease…and that's a fact.

Bronchitis, emphysema, cough, and cancer—
Tell me your symptoms, I'll give you the answer.
Those cool-looking papers you hold with your lips
Don't care if you've got fancy long filtertips.

They still have the power to act in your Lungs
Like a thousand Medusas with nicotine tongues,
To ruin the lining of bronchi and cells,
And hasten the tolling of funeral bells!

If you want to appear like a cool dude, just smoke!
Cough up phlegm, spit loogies, and try not to choke!
And someday you'll have the great honor, in turn,
To have your own ashes end up in an urn.

Laparoscopist – Surgeon who doesn't like blood on his hands

Legal Medicine – Opposite of Illegal medicine.

Licensed Practical Nurse – Woman whose favorite book is *One Flew Over the Cuckoo's Nest*

Liver Doctor – See Hepatologist; see Julia Child's Cookbook with onions

My If you're going to get Malaria,
Be sure you're in a civilized country
Where someone will take caria!

Military Doctor – A physician who can retire after twenty years and likes military music

Medical Student – A high-minded naïf who still believes in the legacy of Albert Schweitzer

McCoy – Renowned physician of *Star Trek* fame, who heals with a beeper

JOEL BERMAN

If *A Farewell to Arms* wasn't prose, but in verse,
We'd have a great poem about a young Nurse.
But Hemingway opted for lines that don't rhyme,
So we'll have to praise Nurses at this place and time.

In my estimation, they all got bum raps
When they stopped putting on those little white caps.
The problem arose when some nurses were male,
(Or didn't you know about Sam Nightingale?).

The Annals of Nursing have forgotten about
Florence's brother, a reckless old lout,
Who had a conversion experience at eighty,
When his life was saved by a Nurse named O'Grady.

From that moment on, he emptied his purse,
Went to school and became a premier male Nurse.
But he looked rather silly in a peakèd white hat,
So he changed his chapeau to a beret that was flat.

And now, when I think with sad longing of Nurses,
Whose hats have inspired me to write all these verses,
I picture old Sam in a wheelchair, quite slick,
Tending to patients who all look quite sick.

So to put the romance back in Nursing, I plan
To recommend change for each woman and man.

All nurses should paint their left ears lily white,
And we'd all be able to know them on sight.

When patients saw nurses, they'd drop all their fears.
It would give a new meaning to *Lend me your ears!*
And whether you're American or whether you're foreign,
We'll know by your ears that, for sure, you're an R.N.

Nephrologist – A euphemism for Wee Wee doctor

Neurologist – Son of an old-rologist

Neurosurgeon – See Brain surgeon

Neurotic Doctor – Same as Physician

Normal Doctor – A misnomer

O

If you have over-active Ovaries,
You may have troubles, like Madame Bovary's.

Obstetrician – A kindly doctor who doesn't own a bed and therefore spends nights in the hospital

Oculist – A Southern compendium of high I.Q. people

Oncologist – See Cancer Specialist

Ophthalmologist – As would be expected, one of the longest names for the specialist with the smallest organ; someone who keeps an eye out for you

Optometrist – A man with a rosy outlook on life, through a new pair of glasses

Oral Surgeon – Opposite of Anal Surgeon

Orthopedist – Physician with fractured sense of humor

Osteopath – Well-worn route to the bottom of the Grand Canyon

P A very remarkable subject is Pain.
When we do something foolish, it makes us refrain
From repeating the process, and yet we complain,
So we just do it over and over again!

Now I heard from some biblical scholars a rumor
That God really has a bizarre sense of humor,
To make such a thing as a painful reaction
Whenever we do an injurious action.

But, then, there is pain when you've got a disease,
Which leads to a doctor collecting his fees.
The rabbis and priests ask the Lord for his blessing,
But it often won't help; it is just window dressing.

There are twinges and smarting, stabbing and aches,
Soreness and throbbing and gnawing…land sakes.
There are more types of pain than I care to repeat,
And they're brought on by illnesses, wounds, ice, or heat.

But I have the answers to all of your Pains,
Transcribed from a treatise discovered by Thanes,
And I'll give them all to you…for a payment quite fair…
I accept cash and credit…but not Medicare.

Pathologist – Similar to osteopath…but with a medical degree

Pediatrician – One who reads mystery books by P. D. James

Penologist – Viagra salesman

Personal Doctor – Physician to the rich and famous, who specializes in narcotics and amphetamines

Pharmacologist – Rural doctor

Physiologist – Specialist with Sloe Gin

Plastic Surgeon – Doctor who does not use plastic; false advertiser

Preferred Provider – A provider of care that no one prefers

Primary Doctor – A physician wined and dined by specialists in order to get referrals

Prison Doctor – What a judge says to a physician who has committed a felony

Private Doctor – A dying-out breed, akin to the California condor

Psychiatrist – A man who needs psychiatric help

Pulmonary Doctor – A physician who practices on a train

Q is for the doctor (we all should bring him back),
The kindly, effervescent, dear, and loving family Quack.
He never really harmed a soul (a few got mortis rigor).
He had a bedside manner that could tranquilize a tiger.

His potions, mostly alcohol, made dowagers feel better,
And bottles painted red and black were offered by the letter.
Potion A was good for hives, and B was good for cancer.
C and D ate up T.B., and E a breast enhancer.

Come rain or shine, he always had a fancy, bottled liquid.
He never let you down and always gave you pills to stick wid.
He never was a pedant, and for manners did not lack.
Please, someone help me find, and then bring back, our
    family Quack!

Quack – An unnecessary adjunct to the medical profession; a scoundrel who endears, then cheats, sick people

Quincy – Another television doctor who leaps tall buildings in a single bound and is allegedly more powerful than a speeding locomotive

Qualified Specialist – A physician who drives a Rolls Royce

Rhinorrhea, I suppose,
Is when I need to blow my nose.
I always have a box of Kleenex,
So…nothing ever runs between us.

If kids have allergies at camps,
They'll be the best nose-running champs.
If they have nasal diarrhea,
Remember…it's called Rhinorrhea!

And if you think this poem's a pip,
You should see the one on postnasal drip!

Radiation Therapist – An M.D. who works at the beach in the summertime

Radiologist – One step up from a crystal ball gazer

Rectal Surgeon – Physician with crappy job

Rheumatologist – Doctor specializing in disreputable joints

Roentgenologists – Radiologists who want to feel special by using a big name

Raskolnikov, Rodion Romanovich – Fictional inept, neurotic murderer in Dostoevsky's *Crime and Punishment* (who has nothing to do with medicine and whom I have added to this list because I am the writer and can do anything I please in this book)

She don't think I have ever seen,
A lyric line about the Spleen!
And if I were a Splenic cell,
I surely would be mad as hell!

'Cause I spend time with my Splenic team,
Keeping your blood system young and clean.
And if I rupture, at any age,
I cause a lot of hemorrhage.

So give your Spleen its due respect.
How 'bout a Splenic genuflect?

Surgeon – Licensee of the school of arrogance

Senile Doctor – Egyptian physician

Seuss, Dr. – Pen name of Theodor Seuss Geisel who revolutionized medicine using potions such as *Green Eggs and Ham, One Fish, Two Fish, Red Fish, Blue Fish* in his peculiar diet, which was effective in treating child depression

Sex Doctor – Question asked of handsome young doctor by lonely patient

Specialist – A label to increase remuneration

Spine Surgeon – A man who uses cacti for cure

Spock, Dr. Benjamin – Pediatrician whose book sold more than 50 million copies, second in sales only to the Bible

Sports Medicine Doctor – A physician who gets free tickets to major sporting events

Staff Doctor – Physician described in Psalm twenty-three, who also holds a rod for God to comfort patients

If Tongues were not invented, we
Would not be able to say *L* and *T*.
Tit for tat would be "ih for ah,"
And all we could say would be "I wuv you, ma!"

And what would we do for the famous French kiss?
The lips might touch…but the mouths would miss!
Thank heaven for this organ with which we can speak,
Without it we'd never say things… *tongue in cheek!*

Teaching Doctor – A physician who can't make a living in private practice

Thoracic Surgeon – Prime rib doctor without spare ribs

Toxicologist – M.D. who drives a cab

Trauma Surgeon – A doctor who attempts to do something when a person falls off a twenty-story building

Tropical Medicine Doctor – Albert Schweitzer wannabe

U

I think we should be proud to note,
That little thing hanging in your throat.
Doctors look at it when it's red,
Which means you ought to stay in bed!

The Uvula, as this thing is known,
Never changes, once it's finally grown.
It seems to have a dull existence,
Giving no breathing or swallowing assistance.

It must be left over from some other organ
That God was creating, that long ago mornin'.
And though He had meant to discard it that day,
It fell in the throat, and there it would stay!

So now it just hangs around, welcoming air,
And gazing at food as it passes by there.
So...if contemplation of your navel will no longer move ya,
Open your mouth and wave at your Uvula!

Urologist – Not my rologist

Uncle Fred – Relative who is not a physician, but has an answer for every medical problem

For flu and colds, or just to tire us,
We have the ubiquitous evil…the Virus!
There are hundreds of strains and many diseases,
And the damn little thing does just as it pleases!

They all have a nucleic acid that drives 'em,
Either R- or D-NA describes 'em.
Now, the polio Virus was wiped out by Salk,
But now there is AIDS, which gets all the talk.

And I am quite certain, like a surgeon's suture,
We'll tie up the problem in the very near future!
In the meantime, stay healthy, so others will hire us,
And certainly don't let the Virus acquire us.

Vascular Surgeon – A surgeon who tries to put on a good operating show before amputating a limb

Veterinarian – A doctor who doesn't accept insurance

Virologist – Drs. Salk and Sabin. Are there any others? A doctor who knows every answer and always knows vi

Thomas Willis, an Oxford professor in sixteen sixty-four,
Described the arteries in the brain as well as a whole lot more.
Myasthenia gravis and childbed fever were named by him during that time,
(The only reason I added these facts was to finish this part of the rhyme!)

The arteries carrying the blood to the brain (to cut one would certainly kill us),
All join with each other in one giant loop, which is known as the Circle of Willis.
So now, with friends at a soirée (when you are talking together),
You can expound on the Circle of Willis instead of discussing the weather!

Writer/Doctor – The last refuge of a tired doctor

Wise Old Doctor – Unknown, extinct species, like the Dodo or Passenger Pigeon

X

Conrad Roentgen, in a daze,
Discovered some strange electrical rays.
And poised between O and X (hugs and kisses),
He chose the X; he loved kissing his missus!

So X-rays were born, and we use 'em in tests,
To see lungs, intestines, the brain, and the breasts.
But had he been more into hugging that day,
We'd probably be calling it now…the O-ray!

X-ray Doctor – See radiologist

X, Dr. – Unknown doctor who is responsible for most of the mistakes made in medicine

Yof genetic materials, if anyone cares,
We're given, from birth, just twenty-three pairs.
Most of them, we know, are called autosomes,
But just two are known as the sex chromosomes.

Now, if you're a woman, then you have two X's,
But remember we're dealing with two different sexes!
Men have one X, but it may make them cry,
'Cause their poor stunted second is what we call Y.

The female egg always has just one X,
But a sperm's X or Y determines the sex.
So if you're a male, you can just close your eyes,
And thank the dear Lord for making the Y's.

Young Doctor – Television actor making ten times the salary of a licensed physician

Y Doctor – Question often posed by patients to their physician and probably named after some ancient Neolithic healer, Doctor Y

Believe it or not, there's a Zonule of Zinn,
Which determines the position your eye lens is in.
This suspensory ligament of the lens
Is as strong in women's eyes as it is in the men's.

When you see a fellow making eyes at a girl,
He's just letting his ligaments coil and unfurl.
If your date's getting boring and you need a line in,
Just tell her she turns on your Zonule of Zinn!

Zoologist – Retired physician who takes his grandchildren on outings